"What a wonderful and creative idea to write a children's book on Joel, reminding us that all of Scripture is for all ages and for all times. The story is relayed simply and elegantly, and the drawings are nothing short of amazing as they communicate the message of Joel in another dimension. I am grateful for this beautifully illustrated rendition of Joel's message for children and for all of us."

— Thomas Schreiner,
James Buchanan Harrison Professor of New Testament Interpretation & Professor of Biblical Theology,
The Southern Baptist Theological Seminary

"Children love stories and there is good reason for that—this whole world is telling a story. It's that very story, that very narrative, that is so wonderfully described and illustrated in this beautiful little book. I'm sure it will prove a great resource to parents and a great blessing to their children."

— Tim Challies,
Blogger at challies.com

"Not just an ordinary book for children! Atkinson has a gift to put an ancient book like Joel into plain and simple English so that not only will children understand, but adults as well. The rendering is not only faithful to the original text but puts Joel within the storyline of the Bible as a whole enabling all to grasp its powerful message and rhetoric."

— Peter Gentry
Donald L. Williams Professor of Old Testament Interpretation at
The Southern Baptist Theological Seminary

THE DARKEST DAY

The Good News in Joel

Jonny Atkinson

Illustrated by Caitlin Blaylock

GOSPEL GROWN
Louisville, Kentucky

The Darkest Day: The Good News in Joel

Copyright © 2020 by Jonathan Atkinson
Illustrations copyright © 2020 by Caitlin Blaylock

Published by
Gospel Grown
Louisville, KY
www.gospelgrown.org

Hardcover ISBN: 978-1-7336615-8-4

Scripture quotations are from the ESV® Bible (The Holy Bible, English Standard Version®), copyright © 2001 by Crossway, a publishing ministry of Good News Publishers. Used by permission. All rights reserved.

Printed in the PRC

Jonny Atkinson:

For Walter
May you be among the survivors in
Mount Zion on that Day

Caitlin Blaylock:

For Addie and Ellie

תנך

THE EMMAUS ROAD

Series Introduction

Have you ever wondered what the Old Testament is all about? Do you find yourself reading the New Testament more than the Old? Isn't the New Testament all about Jesus and the Old is now outdated?

Jesus taught that the Old Testament is actually all about Him (John 5:39). He said that many important things in His life happened to fulfill the Scriptures (Matthew 26:54, John 19:36, etc.). But even Jesus' disciples found this hard to understand. After Jesus died and rose again, He appeared to two of His disciples walking on the Emmaus Road. On that road, Jesus declared again that all parts of the Old Testament were fulfilled in His life. But at that time Jesus also "opened their minds to understand the Scriptures" (Luke 24:44–45). From then on, Jesus' followers have been spreading the good news that Jesus died for our sins *in accordance with* the Scriptures (1 Corinthians 15:3).

Paul reminds us that "all Scripture is breathed out by God and profitable" (2 Timothy 3:16). And Jesus welcomed the little children to come to Him (Matthew 19:14). We understand this to mean that Jesus wants children to learn about Him—and that includes learning about Jesus from *all of Scripture*, including the Old Testament.

The Emmaus Road is a series of illustrated children's books that unpacks the message of biblical books from the Old Testament while also showing how these books point to the good news about Jesus Christ. Our prayer is that, through reading these books, God may open the minds of many children to understand the Old Testament and how it points to Jesus so that their knowledge and love of God would increase.

TABLE OF CONTENTS

ALAS FOR THE DAY!

FOR THE DAY OF THE LORD IS NEAR,

AND AS DESTRUCTION FROM THE ALMIGHTY IT COMES.

JOEL 1:15

PART ONE:
RUIN

There once was a prophet named Joel. He lived in the land of Israel with God's people. In his days a terrible locust plague had come and destroyed the crops in the land, and there was a terrible drought in the land which made the ground as hard as stone.

God sent Joel to tell His people that He had sent the locusts and the drought to punish them for their sins. Joel told them that they needed to turn back to God, and quickly, because things were about to get much worse.

A terrifying and dark day was coming when God would punish all people, and no-one would survive that day. Joel said that the people's only hope of escape was to turn back to God right away and ask for His forgiveness. Maybe, just maybe, God would hear His people's cry and turn away from His plan to destroy them.

Joel said to the people, "Listen up everyone! Look at how the locusts have eaten all of our crops! This is like the locust plague that God sent on the Egyptians when He rescued our ancestors from Egypt— only now God has sent the locusts on us!

"Don't tell stories about the locust plague in Egypt any more but tell your children and your grandchildren about this locust plague with which God has punished us!"

(JOEL 1:1–4)

"Wake up you wine-drinkers and weep! Look! There is no more wine left for you because the vines have been destroyed!

"Locusts have come into our land like a strong and mighty army. They have destroyed all our grape vines and fig trees like a vicious lion with sharp teeth."

(JOEL 1:5–8)

8

"You priests need to listen to me too! Cry out loud because you have no more grain or wine left to make offerings to our God!"

(JOEL 1:9)

"Even the ground is crying out because it has no water! All grain, fruit, and oil have been completely destroyed! Look at the farmers and the vineyard workers weeping because their harvest is gone!"

JOEL 1:10–12

"Our punishment is so severe! Our calamity is catastrophic! Everything everywhere is completely destroyed.

"And worst of all, our joy and happiness has been taken away."

(JOEL 1:12)

"Listen. All of this has happened as a punishment for our sins! We have turned away from God!

"God told us this would happen, but He has also told us what we now must do.

"Priests, put on sackcloth, come to the temple, and spend the night before the altar crying out to God!

"Call all the people of the land to come to the temple and to cry out to God for mercy.

"For things are about to get much worse if we do not repent—the Day of the Lord is coming, a terrifying and dark day!"

(JOEL 1:13–14)

"Do you not see what our sins have done? They have ruined our food and taken away all our happiness. We have nothing left. Even the sheep and cows are thirsty and hungry, and are crying out to God for help!"

(Joel 1:15–20)

...Spare your people, O LORD,

and make not your heritage a reproach,

a byword among the nations.

Why should they say among the peoples,

"Where is their God?"

Joel 2:17

PART TWO:
REPENTANCE

"Look out! Beware! The Day of the Lord is about to come! Sound the alarm! Blow the trumpet from God's holy mountain!

"That day will turn to darkness when the Lord sends out His army to carry out His plan to punish His people!"

(Joel 2:1–2)

23

"God's warriors run like wild horses, they sound like speeding chariots, and they destroy beautiful lands and turn them into a desert.

"They get in battle formation and never flinch. Everyone who sees them turns as white as a sheet and trembles with fear!"

(Joel 2:3–9)

25

"On that day, no-one will survive.

"The whole earth will shake, the sun and moon will turn to black, and the stars will stop shining."

(JOEL 2:10–11)

"But— are you listening? Hear what the Lord our God says to us even now:

'There is still time left, turn back to me and weep over your sins. Let your heart be broken over the evil you have done.'

"Did you hear that? Let us turn back to God because He is gracious and merciful, slow to anger and abounding in steadfast love, and able to turn away from sending this punishment on us.

"Who knows? Maybe He will forgive us, and turn away from punishing us for our sins, and send our crops back, and restore our joy!"

(JOEL 2:12–14)

"So, quick, get all the people together! Let no-one be missing. There's no time to waste! Stop whatever you are doing and come to the temple and plead with God. Let us weep over our sins and ask God to spare us, and not to destroy us.

"Let us say together:

'Save us and show how great you are among the nations, Oh God!'"

(JOEL 2:15–17)

THEN THE LORD BECAME JEALOUS FOR HIS LAND

AND HAD PITY ON HIS PEOPLE.

JOEL 2:18

PART THREE:
RESTORATION

D o you know what happened? God heard His people cry out to Him. And God's affection for His people and for His land grew strong and He said to them:

'Do not be afraid. No enemy will harm you. I will drive the enemy into the sea.

'Do not be afraid. I am sending you lots of rain and you will have so many crops they will overflow!'

"Let us say together:
'Rejoice, because the Lord has done great things for us His people!'"

(JOEL 2:18–21)

'I will send the rain. The trees and the fields will flourish once again with fruit and crops. There will be food for you and all the animals.

'Your wine vats will overflow, and your barns will be bursting at the brim! All the years that the locusts took from you I will restore to you.

'You will be full of food and gladness, and you will praise my name. And when I do all this, you will know that I am God, there is no other, and that I live among you.'

(Joel 2:22–27)

'And after I pour out the rain, I will pour out

my Spirit on all people!

'Both sons and daughters will prophesy about me! Both old and young men will see dreams and visions! I will pour out my Spirit on both the male and female servants!'

(JOEL 2:28–29)

God made amazing promises to His people because they turned back to Him with their whole heart.

Joel told the people that, while they may have delayed the day for now, "The Day of Lord is still coming—that great and terrifying day! The dark day when the sun will turn to black and the moon to blood."

But now Joel could say to them, "All who cry out to the Lord will escape and be saved from that day. All whom God calls will survive and be safe on His holy mountain."

(JOEL 2:30-32)

'On that day, I will restore everything that was lost to my people; but I will bring down all my enemies to a valley and judge them for the evil things they have done.'

(Joel 3:1–8)

'Tell my enemies to get ready for battle! They will need everyone they have to fight! Let them come down to the valley to fight where they will meet my warriors and be judged!

'On the Day of the Lord, all peoples of the earth will be in the valley of judgment.'

(JOEL 3:9–15)

"And then the Lord will roar from His holy mountain and judge all peoples, destroying the wicked forever. The earth will shake and the sun turn to black. But He will protect His people who will be safe on His holy mountain."

(JOEL 3:16)

'On that day, you will know that I am the Lord God who lives on His holy mountain.

'And after that day, there will never be anything evil ever again in the world. Every wrong will be made right. And my land will be beautiful and full of people and full of good things.'

(JOEL 3:17–21)

49

The sun and the moon are darkened, and the stars withdraw their shining...
and the heavens and the earth quake. But the Lord is a refuge to his people...

JOEL 3:15-16

Now from the sixth hour there was darkness over all the land until the
ninth hour...And Jesus cried out again with a loud voice and yielded up his
spirit... And the earth shook, and the rocks were split.

MATTHEW 27:45–51

For "everyone who calls on the name of the Lord will be saved."

ROMANS 10:13 / JOEL 2:32

PART FOUR:
JESUS AND JOEL

Joel's message was that a day was coming, a terrifying and dark day, when God would punish people for their sins. Joel told people to "repent, for the Day of the Lord is near!" so that God might spare them and they would be safe on that coming day.

A long time after Joel spoke these words, God the Father sent His Son Jesus into the world. Jesus came and proclaimed a message similar to Joel. He said, "Repent for the Kingdom of Heaven is near!"

Jesus was sent by God to rescue people from the Day of the Lord, that terrifying and dark day when all people would be punished for their sins.

When Jesus died on the cross, the sun turned to black and the earth shook. When Jesus died on the cross, He was punished by God for the sins of His people. When Jesus died on the cross, He experienced that dark and terrifying day so His people would not have to.

Now, for all who trust in Jesus, God will restore all that they had lost because of their sin. But God does not pour out rain so they would have lots of crops, and fruit like He did in the time of Joel.

Now God pours out His Holy Spirit upon all people who trust in Jesus, young and old, boys and girls, just as Joel promised.

There is still a future Day of the Lord coming, when all peoples of the earth will be judged by God. But for those who trust in Jesus, they will be protected by God on that future day.

Everyone in the world is a sinner including you. And so, everyone deserves to be punished by God for their sin. There is a day coming, a dark and terrifying day, when God will punish all people for their sin. But all who turn back to God and cry out to Him to be rescued will be saved. And on that future day, God will keep them safe from all harm.

That day is coming. It is getting closer. Have you turned back to God and asked God to save you? Has God poured His Holy Spirit on you?

Scripture Index

The book of Joel is a literary masterpiece. Through the book of Joel, God continued to reveal His plan of salvation to His people in the Old Testament. God's plan included saving sinners who repent because of His gracious character so that He might dwell among His people forever in a beautiful world. Joel's message often uses the language of many other Old Testament passages to enrich his prophecy with rhetorical, and sometimes ironic, depth. As God's plan of salvation was fulfilled in the work of Jesus Christ, the New Testament authors often used the language of Joel to describe Jesus' death, the gift of the Holy Spirit, and Jesus' second coming. Below are some of the passages from the Old Testament which Joel alludes to and some of the passages in the New Testament that draw upon the language in the book of Joel.

Key Old Testament Passages

Exodus 10:1–6
Exodus 32–34
Deuteronomy 28:38, 51
Deuteronomy 30:1–10
I Kings 8:35–53
Isaiah 13:1–13
Isaiah 24:1–23
Jeremiah 30–33
Psalm 78:4–8, 46–47
Psalm 105:28–34
Psalm 126:1–6

Parallel Verses in the Minor Prophets

Amos 1:2 » Joel 4:18
Obadiah 17 » Joel 2:32
Jonah 3:9 » Joel 2:14
Zephaniah 1:15 » Joel 2:2
Malachi 3:2 » Joel 2:11

New Testament Passages

Matthew 24:29 » Joel 2:10
Matthew 27:45 » Joel 2:2
Acts 2:17–21 » Joel 2:28–32
Romans 10:13 » Joel 2:32
Revelation 6:12–17 » Joel 2:31, 3:15
Revelation 9:7–9 » Joel 1:6, 2:4–5

Note to Parents and Caregivers

It can be tempting to think that the message of an Old Testament book is archaic. What can a book, written over 2500 years ago, have to say to us today? But the Bible is not like any other book. All Scripture is breathed out by God Himself (2 Tim 3:16) and its words are alive and active (Heb 4:12) to accomplish God's purpose (Isa 55:11). One of God's major purposes for His Word is to make people wise for salvation (2 Tim 3:15). In other words, through reading the Old Testament God's message of salvation can literally come alive and cause people to be born again (1 Pet 1:23).

What is the Old Testament all about? Jesus said the Old Testament is all about Him (John 5:39). Paul also said that Jesus died in accordance with the Old Testament Scriptures (1 Cor 15:3). The central message of the Old Testament is no different from the New. It tells, from multiple different angles, God's plan to save people by His grace, a plan which was fulfilled in the life of Jesus Christ.

Joel's message is no different. Joel tells how sin ruins our lives and brings God's punishment upon us. But Joel also tells that God will graciously restore those who repent—that is, those who turn back to God—and ask Him to rescue them. And God's salvation is not for a moment but is forever and includes the complete transformation of people and the world in which they live. In other words, Joel tells the good news that those who repent will be saved not by works but by God's grace.

The Darkest Day illustrates and faithfully retells this good news of God's grace to save from the book of Joel. In reading this book, think of ways that disobedience in your child's life has brought some element of ruin into their life. Then tell them about the merciful God who can take away His punishment when people repent with their whole heart. And not only that, but He will keep them safe forever, He will graciously restore all that they lost, and He will abundantly bless them to overflowing in the world to come.

Hear the good news in Joel, all who call upon the name of the Lord will be saved. (Joel 2:32)